Beast Feasts

Anita Ganeri

Explorer Challenge

Find out whose
tongue this is …

OXFORD
UNIVERSITY PRESS

Contents

Who Eats What?

Animals need food so they can live and grow.

Some animals only eat plants.
They are called herbivores.

Some animals only eat meat.
They are called carnivores.

Some animals eat plants and meat.
They are called omnivores.

Herbivores

This moth uses its long tongue to suck up the sweet **nectar**.

Koalas mainly eat just one kind of leaf. The leaves have a strong smell. The koalas eat so many leaves that they smell, too.

An elephant picks up leaves, fruit and bark with its trunk. It puts them into its mouth.

This giant tortoise likes leaves, grass and **cacti**. It has no teeth. It bites with its hard, sharp mouth.

Carnivores

A deep-sea angler fish has a light above its mouth. In the dark water, fish swim to the light. The angler fish gobbles them up.

A sand cat hunts by digging. It catches **rodents**, birds and snakes.

Komodo dragons eat animals like deer. They tear the meat with their teeth.

The blue whale is the biggest animal that has ever lived. It eats tiny sea animals, called krill.

Omnivores

Chameleons use their long, sticky tongues to catch insects. This chameleon also eats plants.

A toucan has a big, bright **bill** for picking fruit. Toucans also eat insects and birds' eggs.

An aye-aye eats fruit and insect **grubs**.
It pulls grubs out of trees with its finger.

Giant pandas love **bamboo**. If there's no bamboo, they eat birds and rats.

Some humans eat meat, fish, fruit and vegetables. They are omnivores.

Some people do not eat meat, fish, eggs or milk. They are herbivores.

What do you eat?

Glossary

bamboo: a giant grass with tall stems and small leaves

bill: a bird's beak

cacti: plants with thick stems that grow in hot, dry places

grubs: tiny animals that will grow into insects

nectar: a sweet liquid in flowers

rodents: animals with large front teeth to bite food, such as rats and mice

Index

Look Back, Explorers

What does a carnivore eat?

Can you name an animal that eats plants?

The toucan's bill is *big* and *bright*. Can you think of another word to describe it?

Can you describe how the aye-aye catches grubs?

Did you find out whose tongue this is?

Explorer Challenge: a chameleon's tongue (page 16)

What's Next, Explorers?

Now you have read about what these beasts eat, go on a magic key adventure to meet a mystery beast ...

The Strange Beast

Series created by Roderick Hunt and Alex Brychta

OXFORD

Explorer Challenge
for *The Strange Beast*

Find out what the bird eats ...